dad

jokes

every

38-year-old

dad

should

know

MW01233312

Introduction

Just because you're a 38-year-old dad doesn't mean you shouldn't be improving your dad jokes game.

This excellent book of dad jokes is, at the same time, both pretty punny and pretty awful. Now you can be a perfect pain in the neck at the next family gathering or party when you spring these bad dad jokes on everyone.

But why wait until then? These great one-liners and wordplay jokes are perfect for the dinner table, a long car ride with kids, business meetings, toasts, or when you want to impress (or not impress) the people around you.

Read these jokes straight through, skip around, or play the ***Try Not To Laugh Dad Jokes*** game on the next page.

Every good dad knows – bad dad jokes are just how you and eye roll!

Try Not To Laugh Game Rules

Easy Version

1. Find an opponent or split up into two teams.
2. Team 1 reads a joke to Team 2 from anywhere in the book.
3. The person reading the joke looks right at the opposing person or team and can use silly voices and funny faces if they wish.
4. If Team 2:

 Smiles -
(You see lip movement!)
You get
1 point

 Grins -
(You see teeth!)
You get
2 points

 Laughs -
(You hear noise!)
You get
3 points

5. Read one joke at at time, then switch the giving and receiving teams.
6. The team with most points after five rounds wins! Use the score sheets on the following pages.

Challenge Version

1. Same rules apply except you get one point if you can make the other team laugh. No points for smiling or grinning.

Good luck and try not to laugh!

SCORE SHEET

	TEAM 1	TEAM 2
ROUND 1		
ROUND 2		
ROUND 3		
ROUND 4		
ROUND 5		
TOTAL		

	TEAM 1	TEAM 2
ROUND 1		
ROUND 2		
ROUND 3		
ROUND 4		
ROUND 5		
TOTAL		

	TEAM 1	TEAM 2
ROUND 1		
ROUND 2		
ROUND 3		
ROUND 4		
ROUND 5		
TOTAL		

	TEAM 1	TEAM 2
ROUND 1		
ROUND 2		
ROUND 3		
ROUND 4		
ROUND 5		
TOTAL		

	TEAM 1	TEAM 2
ROUND 1		
ROUND 2		
ROUND 3		
ROUND 4		
ROUND 5		
TOTAL		

	TEAM 1	TEAM 2
ROUND 1		
ROUND 2		
ROUND 3		
ROUND 4		
ROUND 5		
TOTAL		

	TEAM 1	TEAM 2
ROUND 1		
ROUND 2		
ROUND 3		
ROUND 4		
ROUND 5		
TOTAL		

	TEAM 1	TEAM 2
ROUND 1		
ROUND 2		
ROUND 3		
ROUND 4		
ROUND 5		
TOTAL		

SCORE SHEET

	TEAM 1	TEAM 2
ROUND 1		
ROUND 2		
ROUND 3		
ROUND 4		
ROUND 5		
TOTAL		

	TEAM 1	TEAM 2
ROUND 1		
ROUND 2		
ROUND 3		
ROUND 4		
ROUND 5		
TOTAL		

	TEAM 1	TEAM 2
ROUND 1		
ROUND 2		
ROUND 3		
ROUND 4		
ROUND 5		
TOTAL		

	TEAM 1	TEAM 2
ROUND 1		
ROUND 2		
ROUND 3		
ROUND 4		
ROUND 5		
TOTAL		

	TEAM 1	TEAM 2
ROUND 1		
ROUND 2		
ROUND 3		
ROUND 4		
ROUND 5		
TOTAL		

	TEAM 1	TEAM 2
ROUND 1		
ROUND 2		
ROUND 3		
ROUND 4		
ROUND 5		
TOTAL		

	TEAM 1	TEAM 2
ROUND 1		
ROUND 2		
ROUND 3		
ROUND 4		
ROUND 5		
TOTAL		

	TEAM 1	TEAM 2
ROUND 1		
ROUND 2		
ROUND 3		
ROUND 4		
ROUND 5		
TOTAL		

My job is to drill holes in things
and then bolt them together.
Boring at first, but later on, it gets riveting!

This week's winning lottery numbers are
5, 13, 17, 23, 29, 37 and 41.
I mean, what are the odds?

I was thinking of running a marathon, but it might be too difficult getting all the roads closed and providing enough water for everyone.

What did the daddy spider say to the baby spider?
"You spend too much time on the web."

I saw a guy flagging down a taxi van today.
I guess you can say he was Van Halen.

I was walking down the street and
this guy was shouting at me, "A, E, I, O, U!"
I thought, *"I'm not going to respond to
that sort of vowel language."*

I just read an article on Facebook about the dangers of
drinking and what it does to your body and I'm not
going to lie, it freaked me out, so that's it!
After today, no more reading.

Why is pasta untrustworthy?
Because some of it is spyghetti.

What do you call a row of people
lifting a block of cheddar?
A cheesy pickup line.

How did the hackers escape?
No idea, they just ransomware!

Why did the can crusher quit his job?
Because it was soda pressing.

I lost 20% of my couch.
Ouch.

I just read Chubby Checker's autobiography.
There's a big twist in the story.

Why did the house go to the doctor?
It was having window panes.

Where do burgers go on New Year's Eve?
To the meat ball.

Nine months isn't really that long.
It just feels like a maternity.

Did you hear the one about the
Easter Bunny who sat on a bee?
It's a tender tail.

I got fired from my job as a taxi driver.
*Turns out customers don't appreciate
it when you go the extra mile.*

What does a termite eat for breakfast?
Oak-meal.

To this day the boy who took my lunch
money at school still takes my money.
On the plus side he makes great Subway sandwiches.

How would you describe the word "atheism"?
A non-prophet organization.

What do you call someone who delivers Indian food?
A currier.

I'm making a new documentary on how to fly a plane.
We're currently filming the pilot.

My son made a dad joke about an axe.
But it just wasn't very cleaver.

I never knew how technologically advanced Moses was.
He had the first tablet that could connect to the cloud.

Did you hear about the first Australian to develop a six pack?
He was an Ab-original.

Yesterday I saw a guy spill all his Scrabble letters on the road.
So I asked him, "What's the word on the street?"

I hate conspiracy theories and I'm convinced there's a group of people out there creating them just to annoy me.

Why was Little Miss Muffet reading a map?
Because she lost her whey!

My bank recently called me to let me
know I had an outstanding balance.
I said, **"Thanks, I used to do gymnastics."**

What do you call a tissue that is sleeping?
A napkin.

What did the game system do when it lost?
It went "Wii, Wii, Wii," all the way home.

What starts with an E and ends
with an E but only has one letter?
An envelope.

What do cloves use for money?
Garlic bread.

I took a video of my shoe yesterday.
It was some very good footage.

Did you hear about the butcher
that sat on his meat grinder?
He got a little behind in his work.

I always keep my guitar in the car now.
It's good for traffic jams.

I bought a dictionary and when I got home
I realized all the pages were blank.
I have no words for how angry I am.

Son: Mentos! Can we get some?
Dad: I already have some Mentos.
Son: Really? Where?
Dad: *On my men feet!*

The guy who stole my diary has died.
My thoughts are with his family.

What happens to department store staff after
wrapping hundreds of gifts at Christmas?
They become bow legged.

Did you hear the one about the geologist?
He took his wife for granite so she left him.

What do you call a half-man and half-horse?
The centaur of attention.

What did the snowman say to the aggressive carrot?
"Get out of my face."

What do you call a one-armed karate man?
A partial artist.

I was asked to go out by four women today!
Turns out I was in the ladies bathroom.

I was going to start a bourbon company,
but I heard it's really a whiskey business.

What do you call a pig with three eyes?
A piiig.

I was drowning in an ocean made
out of orange soda last night.
When I woke up, I realized it was just a Fanta sea.

A girl I'm dating owns a bakery and works long hours.
I don't think it's going to work out.
She's too kneady.

What do you put on an injured pig?
Oink-ment.

My son tried coffee for the first
time today and said it tasted like dirt.
I told him: **It was just ground this morning!**

Welcome to the plastic surgery
addiction support group.
I see a lot of new faces.

How do you get two peaches to fight?
Pit them against each other!

Finding your lost luggage at the airport should be easy.
However, that's not the case.

A blind man walks into a bar...
and a chair, a table, and some people.

Why do Swedish warships have barcodes on them?
So when they dock they can Scandinavian.

The furniture store keeps calling me.
All I wanted was one nightstand!

My friend recently quit his job to
pursue a career in miming.
I haven't heard from him since.

Was the man sad when his flashlight batteries died?
No, he was delighted!

What happened when the man's
tortilla broke off into the salsa?
He abandoned chip.

What does a spy wear on his feet?
Sneakers.

I saw a hippie swimming in the
sea with a shark approaching him.
I shouted to warn him, but he couldn't hear me.
He was too far out, man.

What do you get if you put a duck in a cement mixer?
Quacks in the pavement.

A new type of broom came out,
it is sweeping the nation.

What creature is smarter than a talking parrot?
A spelling bee.

What do you call an
organization that donates places to sit?
A chair-ity.

I tried to cheer my buddy up by inviting him
to a poker night after cows broke into
his marijuana store and ate all his product.
But he couldn't come, the steaks were too high.

I never have trusted stairs.
They're always up to something.

My wife told me she thought we'd have
less arguments if I wasn't so nitpicky.
I told her, I think you mean "fewer" arguments.

I bet no one will see this one coming.

1.

How many tickles does it take to
make an octopus laugh?
Tentacles.

People make such a big deal about vegans,
but I don't get it.
I've never had beef with one.

What kind of exercise do lazy people do?
Diddly squats.

Who was the first president of the laundry room?
George Washing-done.

What do you call a murderer
who poisons your breakfast?
A cereal killer.

A bus station is where a bus stops.
A train station is where a train stops.
On my desk, I have a workstation.

What do you call a laughing motorcycle?
A Yamahaha.

People in Dubai don't like the Flintstones.
But people in Abu Dhabi do!

I was walking in the jungle and I saw a lizard
on his hind legs telling some really excellent jokes.
I turned to the local tribesman and said,
"That lizard's really funny!"
The tribesman replied, "That's not a lizard,
he's a stand up chameleon."

**Isn't it scary that doctors call
what they do "practice"?**

I named my horse Mayo.
Mayo neighs.

The nicest thing you could ever do
for someone is define the word "bargain".
It means a great deal.

I signed up for my company's 401k.
But I'm nervous because
I've never run that far before.

How did the tree feel in spring?
Releaved.

What would you say if you had
breakfast with the Pope?
"Eggs, Benedict?"

Every year Saint Patrick's Day becomes
a bigger and bigger celebration.
I think it might even keep on Dublin.

Mom: How did you sleep last night?
Dad: *I closed my eyes and waited.*

What does Matt Damon do when he
desperately need cheap clothes?
Goodwill Hunting.

How is an ear of corn like an army?
They both have lots of kernels.

A man went into a library and asked
"Do you have any books on shelving?
The librarian said, "Yes, all of them."

Where do you go to learn to make ice cream?
Sundae school.

Why do aunts never get sick?
Because of their auntie-bodies.

What starts with an "O" and ends with
"nions" and sometimes make you cry?
Opinions.

We can't take our dog outside anymore
because the ducks keep attacking him.
Guess that's what we get for buying a purebred dog.

Why did the farmer buy loads of chicks?
They were all going cheap.

I met a vaping vampire from Romania.
He called himself Vlad the Inhaler.

When I was baptized, the priest
wore a fake moustache, nose and glasses.
It was a blessing in disguise.

I have a pet tree.
It's like having a pet dog, but the bark is quieter.

What happened to the wooden car
with a wooden engine and wooden wheels?
It wooden start.

Going to the park without any food, is no picnic.

What do losing marathon runners
with bad footwear suffer from?
The agony of defeat.

A friend of mine has a bank
account only for buying raisins.
It's a currant account.

I was out walking the dogs today and someone
asked me if they were Jack Russells.
I replied, **"No, they're mine!"**

What do you call a taxi made out of vegetables?
A corn on the cab!

I'm thinking about asking my ex wife to remarry me.
**But I'm worried she will think I'm just
after her for my money.**

Me and my friends are in a band called "Comforter".
We're a cover band.

I made a bicycle by folding
up some paper in my desk drawer.
It doesn't move though, it's a stationary bike.

I asked the toy store clerk where the Arnold
Schwarzenegger action figures were.
She replied: **Aisle B, back.**

What did the fisherman say to the magician?
"Pick a cod, any cod."

What happened to the dad's idea of
building beds above each other to save space?
It was debunked.

After a long time, I told my hot coworker how I felt.
Turns out she felt the same way.
So I turned on the air-conditioning.

What do you call pneumonia that's
been around for a while?
Oldmonia.

What kind of hat does a soda pop wear?
Bottle cap.

A scientist says he is making new eyes.
A blind man says, "That's impossible!"
The scientist says, *"You'll see."*

I just got hired at a company
that makes bicycle wheels!
I'm the spokesperson.

How do you make frog legs?
In a croak pot.

My three favorite things are eating my family
and not using commas.

What do you call a computer floating in the ocean?
A Dell rolling in the deep.

I told my wife that it was her turn to shovel and salt the front steps *but all I got was icy stares.*

How do you know when your cat is sick?
When it's not feline well.

A writer approached me today and asked me to help him find his back garden.
I think he lost the plot.

I said to the gym instructor:
Can you teach me to do the splits?
He said: How flexible are you?
I said: *I can't do Tuesdays.*

How do you make the number one disappear?
You just add a "G" and it's gone.

My wife just told me that
Peter Tork of The Monkees was dead.
I said, "No way!"
Now I'm a bereaver.

Did you hear the joke about the shovel?
It's groundbreaking.

What type of blood do you give a pessimistic person?
B positive.

I just got a new job as a street cleaner!
Turns out there's not much training involved,
you just pick stuff up as you go along.

My least favorite color is purple.
I dislike it more than red and blue combined.

You can actually tell the gender of
an ant by dropping it in water.
If it floats, it's boy ant.

What do you call a wolf that has things figured out?
Aware wolf.

What do you call a pig that does karate?
Porkchop.

Just been reading a new
book all about a short ballerina.
"The Girl with the Dragging Tutu."

I think I know Pavlov.
His name rings a bell.

Do you know what elves rely on
during political campaigns?
Propagandelf.

What kind of shoes do frogs wear?
Open toad.

A password looked at itself in the mirror and said,
**"Don't listen to Google. You are a strong, confident
password no matter what they say."**

What do you call a group of musical whales?
An orca-stra.

Son: Dad I really want to work in
the moisturizer industry, what should I do?
Dad: **The best advice I can give you is to apply daily.**

My dad always said, "Find a girl with an embarrassing tattoo and try to convince her to marry you. *She knows how to make bad decisions but is prepared to stick by them.*"

How do trains drink?
They chug.

After hours of waiting for the bowling alley to open, *we finally got the ball rolling.*

Why was it hard to arrange Goliath's funeral?
It was a giant undertaking.

How does Moses make his coffee?
Hebrews it.

Did you hear the price of cologne went up?
A dollar per-fume.

What's the difference between a
politician and a flying pig?
The F.

What do you call an airship made up of lights?
A LED Zeppelin.

*Bread is like the sun, rises in the yeast
and sets in the waist.*

My aunt has had the same washing machine
since her son Callum died 30 years ago.
**I guess washing machines do last
longer with Cal gone.**

You hear about the latest book on poltergeists?
It's flying off the shelves.

Yesterday I saw a police officer
wearing a pilot's uniform.
I thought it was a bit odd.
**Then I realized he was one of those
plane clothes cops.**

We should have known communism wouldn't work,
too many red flags!

It's Christmas Day and Mariah Carey
opens her present.
It's a piece of paper saying she's been
given a piece of residential land
but she isn't impressed stating,
"I don't want a lot for Christmas."

Why did the capacitor kiss the diode?
He just couldn't resistor.

I'm not a fan of big soda.
But I'm very fond of Minnesota.

Why did the doctor accept a new patient?
He figured he might as well give him a shot.

My boss told me that as a security guard,
it's my job to watch the office.
*I'm on season six but I'm not really sure
what it's got to do with security.*

*I relish the fact that you've mustard
the strength to ketchup to me.*

Lost my watch at a party once.
I saw a guy step on it while he was bothering my wife.
I walked up and gave him a piece of my mind.
No one does that to my wife. *Not on my watch.*

I put a cape on my angry wife.
Now she's super angry.

What did the doctor say to the patient
suffering from a bacterial infection?
"Ah, I see you're a man of culture as well."

How do you keep a bull from charging?
Take away his credit cards.

Yesterday a clown held a door open for me.
I thought it was a nice jester.

How did Richard Nixon sleep in the White House?
First he lied on one side, then he lied on the other.

If you run in front of a car you get tired;
if you run behind a car you get exhausted.

My New Year's resolution is to save enough
money to buy myself a Velcro wall.
I'm planning on sticking to it.

Why did the cat run away from the tree?
Because of its bark.

I'm addicted to puns.
You could say I'm depundent on them.

I don't really mind sitting on the
left or right of a rowing boat.
Either oar.

I remember the first time I got a universal remote.
I thought, **"This changes everything!"**

I walked into the biology lab, and
saw my lab partner dissecting an insect.
"Your fly is open," I said.

As a dentist, I only get paid
for each implant I complete.
Nothing dentured, nothing gained.

My construction company failed after a
competitor started a vicious rumor that
I build houses without a foundation.
It was as a baseless accusation.

Did you hear about the actor
who fell through the floorboards?
He was just going through a stage.

I was walking past a farm and a sign said "Duck, eggs". I thought, that's an unnecessary comma.
Then it hit me.

Dad: How much does it cost to buy a large singing group?
Son: A choir?
Dad: **Ok, fine. How much does it cost to "acquire" a large singing group?**

We all know the show is called "Spongebob Squarepants."
But the star is Patrick.

I'm an optimistic pessimist.
I'm positive things will go wrong.

What did one earthquake say to the other?
"Hey, it's not my fault!"

My wife ripped the blankets off me last night!
But I shall recover.

I just yelle, "F, YOU GUYS!" at my students.
I love being a music teacher.

What does a vegetarian zombie like to eat?
A head of cabbage.

A colony of bacteria walks into a bar.
The bartender tells them they're not welcome.
The bacteria say, **"But we're staph!"**

What happens if you cut the
oxygen supply to the king?
There will be no air to the throne.

Last night some thugs threw
Chinese dumplings at my house.
Can you believe such wonton vandalism!

As a prisoner was released from jail,
he shouted, "Yay, I'm free. I'm free!"
A little boy yelled, *"So what I'm four, I'm four!"*

I went to the doctor yesterday
and he says I'm paranoid.
Who else has he told, I wonder?

What do you get when you cross a robot and a tractor
A transfarmer.

What's the difference between
roast beef and pea soup?
Anyone can learn how to roast beef.

Today I learned that humans eat more
bananas than monkeys.
*It's true because I can't remember the
last time I ate a monkey!*

I used to be in a band called "Missing Cat".
You probably saw our posters.

How do witches keep their hair in place?
With scare spary.

What should you do if there are 14 frogs
on your car's back window?
Use your rear window de-frogger.

*I wonder what bed bugs say to each
other before they go to sleep?*

At my last job interview, I was asked
what my greatest weakness was.
I said, Honesty."
The interviewer said, "I don't think
honesty is a weakness."
I replied, *"I really don't care what you think."*

I am giving up drinking for a month.
Sorry that came out wrong.
I am giving up.
Drinking for a month.

My grandfather is 85 and he still doesn't need glasses.
He drinks straight from the bottle!

What do you call it when a bunch of old men clap?
Menapplause.

I dug up a worm for fishing.
It's the end of the line for him.

How do pigs talk to each other?
Swine language.

What kind of fire leaves a room damp?
A humidifier.

My wife said she would stay with me
if I promised to stop singing Oasis songs.
I said, "Maybe."

I have a playlist of songs from Eminem,
the Cranberries and the Peanuts.
I named it the Trail Mix.

How do you get down from an elephant?
You don't, you get down from a goose.

I'll have the turtle soup.
And make it snappy!

Before we were married I gave my wife some sparkling
water and she completely fell in love with me.
I schwepped her right off her feet.

I used to make a dad joke every year.
But now I am not sure if I can continue
this tradition any father.

Made in United States
Troutdale, OR
05/19/2025

31512552R00037